WHAM!

WHAM!

CHRIS CROOKER

Julian Messner

Published by
Simon & Schuster, Inc., New York

Photo credits:
Laurie Paladino, pg. 10; Chris Craymer, Scope/RDR Productions, pgs. 12, 28, 46, 58; Star File, pg. 13; Sipa Press, pgs. 15, 21, 26, 30, 42 (bottom), 47, 49, 52 (top); Allan Ballard, Scope/RDR Productions, pg. 19; Vinnie Zuffante, Star File, pg. 38; Daily Mail/Special Features, pgs. 40, 56; Laura Luongo, Sipa Press, pgs. 42 (top), 45, 55; Philip Ramey, pg. 52 (bottom).
Cover Photograph of Wham! by Chris Craymer, Scope/RDR Productions © Copyright 1985

Photo Research: Amanda Rubin
Copyright © 1985 by Drew Wheeler and 2M Communications, Ltd.

All rights reserved
including the right of reproduction
in whole or in part in any form.
Published by Julian Messner,
A Division of Simon & Schuster, Inc.
Simon & Schuster Building
Rockefeller Center
1230 Avenue of the Americas
New York, New York 10020

JULIAN MESSNER and colophon are registered
trademarks of Simon & Schuster, Inc.
Also available in a Wanderer Trade Paperback Edition.
Manufactured in the United States of America

Library of Congress Cataloging in Publication Data

Crocker, Chris.
  Wham!

  "Discography and videography": p. 63
  Summary: A brief biography highlighting the careers of the two member rock group.
  1. Wham! (Musical group)—Juvenile literature.
2. Rock musicians—England—Biography—Juvenile literature. [1. Wham! (Musical group) 2. Musicians. 3. Rock music] I. Title.
ML3930.W43C7   1985   784.5'4'00922 [B] [920] 85-10572
ISBN: 0-671-60374-4
      0-671-60281-0 (Pbk)

SPECIAL THANKS TO SUZAN COLON,
ANNENE KAYE, AND DAVID KEEPS
FOR ALL THEIR HELP

ABOUT THE AUTHOR

Chris Crocker is a freelance journalist and author who writes about music and the electronic media. A lifelong observer of the pop scene, Crocker has lived in Manhattan since 1977.

CONTENTS

IN STYLE	9
THE BOYS FROM BUSHEY	11
SOUL ON THE DOLE	17
WHAM! (GOES FOR IT!)	22
FANTASTIC	27
MAKE IT BIG	33
INSIDE WHAM!	37
VIDEO WHAM!	44
THE WHAM! IMAGE	50
WHAM! TODAY	54
FUN FACTS	59
VITAL STATISTICS	61
DISCOGRAPHY AND VIDEOGRAPHY	62
WRITE TO WHAM!	64

IN STYLE

Style. It's a hard thing to define. *Style* can be recognized instantly, although *styles* are always changing. There are clothing styles, hair styles, musical styles, and life-styles. You could even say there are as many different styles as there are different people. Nonetheless, styles are always shaped by individuals—a very special few whose *personal* style influences the rest of the world.

George Michael and Andrew Ridgeley of Wham! are two such individuals. Wham! is more than just a pop music group; Wham! is the ultimate expression of style. Their style of dress, their style of music, even their life-styles have made an impact on young people everywhere. George Michael and Andrew Ridgeley became trendsetters the only way they knew how—by just being themselves.

You'll discover how Wham! rocketed out of obscurity all the way to the top of the charts in a matter of months. You'll see how two teenagers with a lot of ideas (and no money) became an international success story, reaching milestones that would make pop history.

On a personal scale, you'll find out that the story of Wham! is the story of the friendship of George Michael and Andrew Ridgeley. Their lifelong partnership proves that two people determined to live out their dreams can do just that, no matter what obstacles lie ahead.

As any video screen, radio, magazine, or newspaper anywhere will attest, Wham! is shaping today's styles. How could two kids from the north of London become such a phenomenon? How, exactly, did Wham! do it? Of course, they did it with *style* . . .

THE BOYS FROM BUSHEY

The year was 1963. In England, that was the year that the Beatles first gained popularity, although they were scarcely known in America. That year, the vast, untapped power of pop music was about to explode as the four musicians from Liverpool rocketed to fame. But in that same year—in other parts of Britain—*something else* was happening that would change the face of pop music forever.

On January 26, 1963, Andrew John Ridgeley was born in Surrey, England. His father is an Egyptian-born executive at a camera company. Andrew grew up in Bushey, a suburb to the north of London, with his little brother Paul. Aside from the obvious cultural differences between England and the United States, Bushey was very much like any other town outside a major city. While families like the Ridgeleys weren't *rich,* they lived quite comfortably, and there was little that Andrew or Paul ever had to do without.

On June 6, 1963, in a hospital in Finchely, England, a boy named George Michael Panos came into the world.

Fans might find it hard to believe that George, as a young boy, wasn't really "hot stuff with the girls."

The son of a Greek Cypriot restaurateur whose name was originally Panayiotou, George has two sisters, Yioda and Melanie. When George was 12, his family moved from Radlett, England to nearby Bushey.

Perhaps someone will put up a plaque at the Bushey Meads School in the county of Hertfordshire, for this was the true birthplace of Wham!. When George started there in the fall of 1975, all the other children in the grade had known each other for a year. He was the shy new boy in class. "I was overweight with puppy fat and I wore thick glasses," George once said. "I knew I wasn't hot stuff with the girls . . ."

By the luck of a seating chart, George sat next to Andrew Ridgeley, who was known to be a bit of a troublemaker. At recess, George and Andrew got acquainted in a novel manner. "There was some kind of

THE BOYS FROM BUSHEY

game in the break," George recalled to *Star Hits*, "you know, where you throw each other off the wall. Well, I threw him off and he hit his head. He was one of the rowdy ones in the class so that was a major breakthrough for me. Everyone respected me after that . . . until they realized it was a fluke! Andrew said something to the effect that if I hadn't been new he would've kicked my head in."

George admired Andrew's taste in clothes and his knowledge of the rock 'n' roll scene. But George's parents thought of Andrew as a bad influence. The two friends spent much of their spare time listening to the radio. Their favorite pop groups at the time were Queen, who had a big hit with "Bohemian Rhapsody," and Elton John, who was topping the charts with "Island

Andrew was a bit of a troublemaker in school.

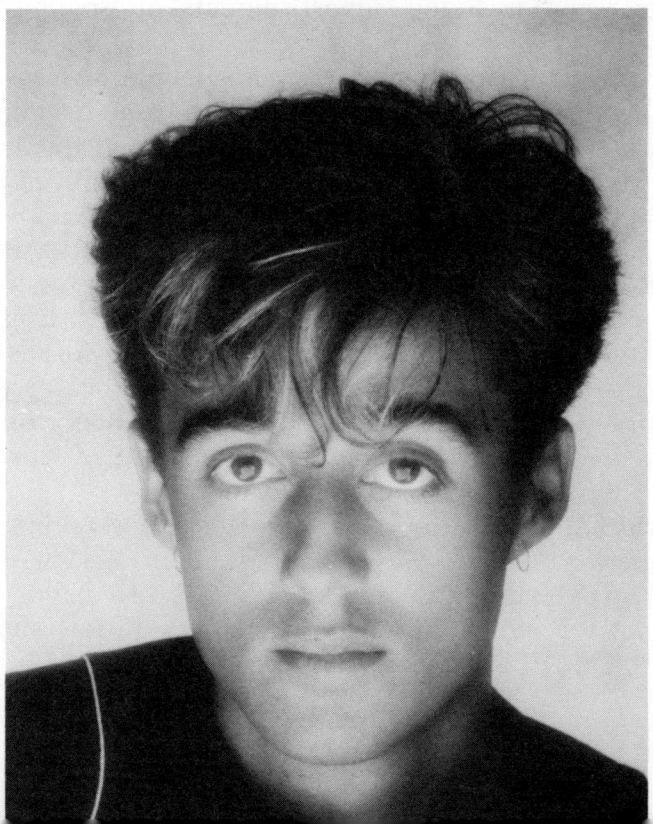

Girl." (Though Elton John is still very popular today, his fame reached its peak in the mid 1970s.)

Even before George met Andrew, he'd aspired to be a pop star. "I'd got the singing bug when I was seven," George once explained in an interview, "and Mum had given me a tape recorder as a present. As I got older, Dad was against the idea but Mum began to realize that I might just have something and started to sympathize with me."

The tape recorder was the perfect outlet for George and Andrew's musical energies. "One of the main reasons we became friends was music," Andrew once remarked. "George had a tape recorder at his house and we used to go over there and thrash things out on his drum kit and an old acoustic guitar." As time went on, their tape experiments would become more elaborate. They even included advertisements on some of the tapes.

Forming a pop band was very much on Andrew's mind at this time—but George was trying to keep his mind on schoolwork. As much fun as a band seemed to George, he knew that his studies were important (even if he wasn't exactly a high-achiever in the classroom).

During their teenage years, George and Andrew worked at a number of low-paying jobs. Andrew would sometimes deejay in the pubs around Watford, England. George had a series of odd jobs—as a worker at a construction site and an usher at a movie theater. Once George was employed by a major British chain store and was fired for not wearing the right kind of shirt and tie—and he worked in the stockroom!

During these same years, upheavals were taking place in the world of pop music. After the Ramones toured the United Kingdom, British kids and British bands went all-out for punk. Groups like the Sex Pistols shocked

English society with their noisy guitars, outrageous lyrics, and wild leather-and-chain outfits.

Still, George and Andrew were unimpressed by their punked-out peer group. Rather than listen to those high-decibel songs, they were happier listening to the smooth sounds of American soul and disco. They dressed in sharp suits and baggy pants that recalled the jazzy hipsters of the 1940s and 1950s. George and Andrew considered themselves "soul boys" at the time, and enjoyed the discos that were far removed from the tumult of the punk clubs.

The epitome of style.

But a shift in the trends of pop music brought about a change in the lives of George and Andrew. In the fall of 1979, British audiences took a great liking to soul artists McFadden and Whitehead's song "Ain't No Stoppin' Us Now." The song was a bit slower than the hard-driving disco that had been so popular. Soon, many club deejays played mostly softer, jazzier soul records that lacked the urgent beat George and Andrew craved.

Drifting away from rhythm and blues, George and Andrew were attracted to the English ska revival. Ska is an extremely bouncy style of West Indian pop music that flourished in the early '60s. In the late '70s, groups like the Specials and Selecter returned to ska and wrote their songs in that style. Ska revival bands were usually made up of white musicians of European descent and black musicians of West Indian descent, and the label "two-tone" was often applied to them. The two-tone idea was one the bands could be proud of, and it was further reflected in their strictly black-and-white outfits.

Ska's frantic dance beat appealed to George and Andrew—so did the elegant simplicity of its two-tone fashions. George had resisted Andrew's pleas to start up a band because he wanted to continue his schoolwork. But just before George was to take his "A" level tests—which are critical for college acceptance—*he changed his mind.*

George and Andrew would form a ska band.

SOUL ON THE DOLE

November 5 is celebrated throughout Great Britain as Guy Fawkes Day. On that day in 1979, George Michael and Andrew Ridgeley founded their first band. They christened themselves The Executives, and the duo wasted no time in starting to write songs. As always, George and Andrew worked together very closely. The three other band members often felt left out, since George and Andrew insisted on running things *their* way.

The Executives never managed to break out of their northern London local scene and into any of the big-time London clubs, but they *did* record a demo tape of their best songs. Demos are usually inexpensively made recordings used to give record companies an idea of what a group sounds like. The Executives' manager took their admittedly crude demos around to any record company that would listen. The demos seemed to have aroused some interest at Arista and Go-Feet Records in London. Exactly *how* much interest they aroused may never be known, because two weeks after the record companies heard their demo tapes, The Executives disintegrated. George recalled their songs in the *New Musical Express:* "A couple of them could've been really big hits. If someone had been clever enough to pick us up, organize us properly, we could've had some really big hits."

In the long run, George and Andrew were wise to drop out of the ska revival—the trend had run its course, and few record companies wanted any more ska groups. George *does* wonder if he made the right decision leaving his tape with Go-Feet Records. A ska version of the old Andy Williams song, "Can't Get Used to Losing You," was included on The Executives' demo. A few months later, Go-Feet recording artists The English Beat scored a hit with an updated version of . . . "Can't Get Used to Losing You"! To George, it looked like more than an accident, but he admits that the two versions of the song are different enough for it to have truly been a coincidence.

Now that George and Andrew were temporarily out of the music business, and permanently out of school, they needed to find work. Since unemployment in Britain has been so severe in the past few years, a great many teenagers receive unemployment checks from the government. This is what George and Andrew did.

Unlike the United States, Britain offers unemployment money to most everyone who isn't working, not just to those who have lost their jobs. To the youth of England, receiving social security benefits is casually known as "going on the dole." Some teenagers search for the few jobs available while others coast along indefinitely on government checks. George and Andrew decided to keep living at home and use the money to launch their next musical project. What *that* would be, neither was sure. The destiny of George Michael and Andrew Ridgeley would once again be linked to the shifting styles of pop music.

Across the Atlantic in New York, the dance clubs and playgrounds of the South Bronx were bursting with a new style of music that called itself rap. Instead of singing their lyrics, rappers call them out with a powerful rhythmic drive. As early as 1978, Kurtis Blow had one of the first smash hits of rap with "The Breaks." Other prominent rap artists include Afrika Bambaataa, The Fearless Four, Grandmaster Flash, and The Furious Five. The new dance music out of New York was tough and aggressive—soon British deejays would fall into rap's new groove.

In 1981, George and Andrew were like many other English teens on the dole. They went back to the discos they'd abandoned a couple of years before, lured by the wild new sounds of American funk and rap artists. A local club that George and Andrew frequented was called Le

Beat Route. One night, while dancing at Le Beat Route, George and Andrew took a cue from the drumbeats coming over the club's PA system and made up a rap song on the spot! With such an outpouring of spontaneous musical inspiration, they knew what direction their music would take.

As in The Executives, George and Andrew wanted to handle everything themselves. "When we were putting our ideas together," Andrew has recalled, "we couldn't find anyone else who was on the same wavelength, anyone else with the same sense of humor. It was easier to stick to a team of just two." By December of 1981, they had made a demo tape of their three new songs: "Wham Rap," "Come On," and "Club Tropicana." "Wham Rap" was really an elaborate version of George and Andrew's impromptu performance at Le Beat Route —and they considered it their best song.

Even a group with only two members needs a name, and Wham! was the name they picked. "We lifted it from our first single, called 'Wham Rap,'" Andrew told *Video Rock Stars*. "We chose the name Wham! because it was short, a short name that was fairly memorable and had a lot of impact. You know, we wanted something that was energetic, youthful. And I think we got that across with it."

Aware of how a badly recorded demo tape can make a group sound forgettable, George and Andrew tried something new with their Wham! demos. The entire tape was just a couple of minutes in length. Instead of simply recording all three songs, they only included a brief snippet of each—as though it were a radio advertisement. How different was that from the old tapes they used to make in George's room?

George has remarked of those earliest days, "We were both convinced that once our songs were heard by the right people, we were going to make it."

At the same time, a man named Mike Dean was forming his own record label called Innervision Records. Previously, Dean had worked at Phonogram Records and signed the group ABC to that label. When Mike Dean got the Wham! demos, he was impressed by what he heard. In March 1982, George Michael and Andrew Ridgeley signed a contract with Innervision Records. Wham! was ready to hit the pop music world head-on.

WHAM! (GOES FOR IT!)

George and Andrew may have taken full control of Wham!'s creative output, but they were at a clear disadvantage as businessmen. Perhaps to cut costs, they thought it best not to pay a manager to handle their business affairs. But any professional musician needs a sharp manager (and it's a rare musician indeed who can assume all the duties of a manager and still have time for music).

Innervision Records gave George and Andrew an advance of around $700 each. In the music industry, this is a pitiably small sum, but George and Andrew were in no position to argue. After all, they did have a contract, and that *was* the hardest battle to win. The two were also encouraged by the fact that Innervision, although a small and new label, had the support of powerful CBS Records.

In April 1982, Wham! entered the studio to record what was already their signature theme, "Wham Rap (Enjoy What You Do)." They hired producer Bob Carter

WHAM! (GOES FOR IT!)

for the single. A producer is responsible for how a record sounds in much the same way as a movie director is responsible for how a movie looks. Bob Carter was a studio veteran who produced records by British soul sensation Junior, so George and Andrew felt he was a good choice. Even as they began recording, their ideas were still evolving. "The song was originally going to be a real parody of a disco rap," Andrew told the *New Musical Express*, "but once we got into the studio, that all changed and we went for a much harder, aggressive sound." By the time "Wham Rap" was completed, George and Andrew felt that Bob Carter hadn't given the record the kind of sound it needed.

When "Wham Rap" was released in June of 1982, the critics on England's influential music weeklies had little positive reaction. It only reached the #91 position on national singles charts—hardly a triumphant debut! George and Andrew say that the company didn't press enough copies of "Wham Rap" to keep the record stores stocked, frustrating their potential audience.

The other explanation for the public's timid reaction to "Wham Rap" was its subject matter. The lyrics describe life on the dole as having a certain glamour, as suggested by a line like: "I'm a soul boy—I'm a dole boy." Many people thought that the song was disrespectful both to the government that pays the tab and also to the honest employment-seekers who wish they could get off the dole. Another view was that the song was meant to *cheer up* the unemployed—after all, George and Andrew wrote it when *they* were on the dole. "It was misconstrued by the press over in London," Andrew later explained. "They were looking for a band that seemed to uphold the same kind of ideals they had. We wrote a song about the dole simply because that was our situation at the time."

Wham! maintains that the key to this controversial song is enclosed in the parentheses—"(Enjoy What You Do)." They say their theme is one of making the best of every situation. As Andrew told *Melody Maker*, "You won't find in any of our interviews that we said the song had any incredible social message."

The summer of 1982 was a low point for Wham! With sales of their single foundering, they attempted a tour to promote the record in person. Since they had no money to hire a band, George and Andrew traveled around lip-syncing to their own tape! The promotional tour had little success.

In July, Innervision Records sent Wham! to New York to let a new producer "remix" the tapes of "Wham Rap (Enjoy What You Do)." Maybe Wham! felt somehow closer to the raw rap roots of the South Bronx, because they were very pleased with the U.S. remix of their first single.

An album's "mix" is the way a recording engineer combines the separate instruments and voices in a particular song. If a song proves to be a dance hit, a group will very often re-enter the studio and "re-mix" the tapes of their original recording sessions for discothèques. A re-mix will usually be longer, and the bass and drum parts will be louder than in the first mix of a song.

The producer was Francois Kevorkian, who had served as producer for funk stars D-Train. Even though George and Andrew liked the new version of "Wham Rap," they didn't feel they could work comfortably with Kevorkian, either. The two then returned to England.

Steve Brown was the producer who brought Wham! into the studio for their second single, "Young Guns (Go for It!)." This second 45 was released in September of 1982. When George and Andrew went out promoting it, they had one of the luckiest breaks of their career.

Wham! was scheduled to appear on "Top of the Pops," one of the most widely watched music programs on British television. George and Andrew danced and lip-synced to "Young Guns (Go for It!)," accompanied by their beautiful friends Dee C. Lee and Shirley Holliman. Some people were so impressed by the way the four of them moved that they thought Wham! was a dance group rather than a musical one.

National television exposure had given Wham! a new lease on life—by the year's end, "Young Guns" rose to #4 on the British national charts. In early 1983, "Wham Rap" was rereleased, this time to the warm reception it had deserved in the first place.

When Innervision asked for a third single, George knew he was under a great deal of pressure to come up with a hit. "I wanted a third single to tie up what we started," George remembered. By the time the new single was done, *three* recording studios had been used, and over $20,000 had been spent. After months of torturous work, "Bad Boys" was released in May of 1983. For George and Andrew, the greatest challenge now facing them would be to make an album.

Dancing with friends Dee C. Lee and Shirley Holliman.

FANTASTIC

Fantastic is the title of the first Wham! LP. Over the several months it took to record the album, George found his creative abilities stretched to their limits. George has always been the songwriter of Wham!—to date, Andrew has only helped out on the lyrics to three songs. George plays bass guitar and keyboards, but feels uncomfortable composing on the guitar. An integral part of George's songwriting process used to involve tape-recording bits and pieces of songs as they came to him, but lately he just keeps the melodies in his head until he can play them in their entirety. *Fantastic* was produced by George and past collaborator Steve Brown.

George is far more concerned with the music he writes than with the words. "We're not really concerned with the lyrics," he remarked to *Zig Zag*. "If our lyrics start to lose some of their individuality it's nothing like as bad as the music deteriorating, whereas I think a lot of journalists can't see that. They concentrate too much on the lyric." In *Wham! In Their Own Words*, Andrew explained further: "We could try and write heavy political lyrics, but we wouldn't get any enjoyment out of it. What it boils down to is the main thing George and I have in common: our sense of humor. That's what interests us and that's what goes down on record."

FANTASTIC

Many critics have questioned Andrew Ridgeley's role in Wham! as that of a comparatively talentless hanger-on, but his true role is as vital as it is hard to define. As the guiding light of George Michael's interest in pop music, Andrew is probably *most* responsible for Wham!'s existence. Andrew's sense of style and sense of fun constantly affect the band's direction. On a much less philosophical level, Andrew is the guitarist for Wham! and has no shortage of musical ability. For George as well as Andrew, *Fantastic* showed everyone what Wham! was made of.

Wham!'s *Fantastic* album celebrates the variety of musical styles that George and Andrew enjoyed as teenaged clubgoers. *Fantastic* starts off with their third single, "Bad Boys," a song that reveals the influence of '70s disco/funk with its skittering guitar accompaniment and bright synthesizer chords. In the same spirit, George and Andrew's theme song "Wham Rap" displays sophisticated studio technique, with a "mix" of added instruments, voices, and sound effects.

The calypso stylings and party atmosphere of "Club Tropicana" are all meant to poke fun at Le Beat Route, Wham!'s old hangout. Le Beat Route had been billing itself as the ultimate dance club, and George reacted by creating the "Club Tropicana," where all the drinks are free and sunbathing is optional!

"Young Guns (Go for It!)" is a rap song that takes a cynical look at young married couples, and is one of Wham!'s most popular early hits. Listeners loved George's rapping and the delicate call-and-response choruses of the female backup singers. George's full vocal range was explored on *Fantastic*, from his breathy

◀*Wrestlers of the world get ready - here we come!*

murmurs on "Nothing Looks the Same in the Light" to his soaring falsetto in "A Ray of Sunshine."

Fantastic was an immediate success—in the truest sense of the word "immediate." While most albums climb the charts over weeks (or sometimes months) before reaching the top, *Fantastic* actually entered the chart at #1!

In the United States, the album jacket referred to George and Andrew as "Wham! UK." Wham! didn't call itself by its proper name because there already *was* an American group that laid claim to the name Wham. The U.S. Wham was willing to change its name for George and Andrew, but it wanted *half a million dollars* for the favor. Although the U.S. Wham eventually settled the matter (for a fraction of the money first demanded), American copies of *Fantastic* are attributed to "Wham! UK."

George and Michael weren't the only Wham! in town - another group in the United States was also calling themselves Wham.

With their debut album an instant smash, George and Andrew's pop music career was taking off. Sadly, their financially inadequate Innervision contract kept them firmly anchored to the ground. George and Andrew were now famous pop stars, but they had little money to show for it. During a Wham! appearance on the pop music show "The Tube," George actually told a nation of viewers *not* to buy their newest record! The record in question was the "Club Fantastic Megamix"—a 12-inch extended-play record of Wham! material that Innervision released against their wishes. They preferred that nobody hear the record than that Innervision make any money on it.

George recalled the Innervision dilemma this way in *Star Hits:* "It was a very bad contract which held us for a long time in a situation where we made very little money. There was no point in carrying on, having more hit singles which were making us bigger success-wise, but more ridiculous financially."

The time was ripe for Wham! to make a smart move. George and Andrew hired a good manager. The man who took charge of Wham!'s shaky finances was Simon Napier-Bell, a longtime rock 'n' roll manager.

Some managers have been known to be as intriguing as the acts they handled—such as Colonel Tom Parker, who masterminded Elvis Presley's climb to stardom. Simon Napier-Bell managed the Yardbirds in the 1960s, glitter-rock hero Marc Bolan in the 1970s, and such groups as Japan and David Sylvain in the 1980s. Napier-Bell saw Wham!'s vast potential, and he knew he could put them on the right track. (Incidentally, Napier-Bell also managed David Austin, a sometime Wham! band member who's been a friend of Andrew's for years. George Michael produced David Austin's solo 45, "Turn to Gold.")

One way out of a contract is to *buy* your way out, and Simon Napier-Bell had quite a few ideas on how to raise money to buy Wham!'s contract. He negotiated a deal in which Fila Sportswear paid Wham! over $60,000 to perform exclusively in their clothes. The styles appealed to George and Andrew, and the money was sorely needed.

When "Club Tropicana" was released as the fourth Wham! single, the newly outfitted George and Andrew launched their 1983 tour of Great Britain. The show itself took a novel approach. Rather than an opening band, Wham! hired a deejay to spin records throughout the tour. When the deejay finished, home movies taken by Andrew's father were shown to amused clubgoers. After the movies, a full Wham! band came out to show audiences the kind of energy they could generate. With this live backup, Wham! could take their message directly to their fans. With the tour to support it, "Club Tropicana" made it to the British top ten.

By early 1984, Wham! had finally earned enough to buy their freedom. Although they were now broke, George and Andrew were happy to say goodbye to Innervision Records. Before long, Simon Napier-Bell had negotiated a sensible deal for the band. From that point on, Wham! would record for Epic Records in the United Kingdom and for Columbia Records in the United States. Now all Wham! needed was to make it big.

MAKE IT BIG

As had always been their desire, Wham! took complete control of their music. Their second album, entitled *Make It Big*, was produced and arranged entirely by George Michael. The actual recording took place over six weeks at the Chateau Minerval, a live-in studio complex at Brignole, in the south of France. Other groups that have made records at Chateau Minerval include Pink Floyd, Yes, the Thompson Twins, and Duran Duran.

WAKE ME UP BEFORE YOU GO-GO

Instantly recognizable from the froggy-voiced *"jitterbug!"* that starts it off, "Wake Me Up before You Go-Go" is Wham!'s greatest song. George dipped heavily into his Motown memories and brought some of the splendid sounds of the '60s right into the '80s. To vintage organ accompaniment, George's snappy lead vocals are hugged by an urgent backing chorus that recalls "girl groups" such as the Supremes or the Marvelettes.

"I'd been thinking of using "Wake Me Up before You Go-Go" as just a *line* in a song," George explained, "and then it came into my head with a tune so I wrote it and decided to release it in the autumn. Then I thought . . . let's do it now!"

The decision to press forward with "Wake Me Up" was sound—aside from being the #1 single in both England and the United States, it raced to the top of the charts in Australia, Belgium, Holland, Norway, Austria, Denmark, and Ireland.

EVERYTHING SHE WANTS

An oversized-sounding blooping synthesizer was a staple of 1970s funk, and it pervades "Everything She Wants." The softer ooh-ooh choruses are much farther in the background than those in "Wake Me Up." This story of expectations and demands in a relationship is haunted by shouts of the word *wham*, barely audible over the percussion.

HEARTBEAT

The second visit to the soulful '60s on *Make It Big* is "Heartbeat." With its clicking castanets and clear, ringing piano chords, it revives the "wall of sound" technique of legendary producer Phil Spector. Spector was the genius behind such early '60s hitmakers as the Ronettes, the Crystals, and Darlene Love. Bruce Springsteen duplicated the Spector sound in his hit "Hungry Heart."

LIKE A BABY

A lazily strummed guitar and shimmering electric piano chords introduce this slow-tempo soul ballad. The mood is serene and gentle as jazzy accents highlight the lush, romantic atmosphere. George croons evocatively, his voice awash with echoes.

FREEDOM
"Freedom" is a solidly written rhythm-and-blues number that sounds as if it is related to the stirring soul anthems of Culture Club or songstress Mari Wilson. Guitars and bass insistently prod the driving dance beat, making the appeal of "Freedom" inescapable. When released as the third single from *Make It Big*, it went—where else?— to #1.

IF YOU WERE THERE
Originally recorded by soulmasters the Isley Brothers in 1973, "If You Were There" gets the George Michael overhaul. Over the clapping percussion track, George's falsetto sails to new heights in this steady dance number.

CREDIT CARD BABY
Underscored by snaky guitar lines, the R&B hop of "Credit Card Baby" has the same kind of irresistibility that made "Freedom" such a hit. Another playful look at modern love, this song is about a guy who'd rather give his credit cards to a woman than his affection.

CARELESS WHISPER
Actually a George Michael solo project, "Careless Whisper" became an international hit in 1984 and 1985. George's plaintive, emotional vocals cut across the electronic string section. Female backup singers chime in like witnessing angels, while a bleating saxophone suggests exotic places and pleasures.

At this point, no one should be surprised that "Careless Whisper" was *the* #1 single in England, the United States, Australia, and many European nations.

Just like *Fantastic* before it, *Make It Big* started on the British charts at the #1 spot. In the United States, *Make It Big* was certified as both a gold* and platinum** album in December of 1984. Although it became the #1 LP in America, a *million copies* of the record had been sold before it even reached the top ten. Wham!'s biggest following may be right here in the U.S.A.!

*A record reaches gold status when 500,000 copies are sold.
**A record reaches platinum status when 1,000,000 copies are sold.

INSIDE WHAM!

With the success of Wham!, George and Andrew became internationally known pop personalities. As their pictures adorned the covers of music magazines, Britain's tabloid press reported their every move. Was there anything special about George and Andrew's background that groomed them for such popularity? Actually, their upbringings were quite conventional.

Mrs. Lesley Panos, George's mother, currently helps out in Mr. Panos' restaurant, but when George was in grade school she worked as a secretary. George remembers fondly how she would never fail to meet him when he got home from school. Still, Mrs. Panos was a fairly strict mother. She didn't punish George physically—except when he *really* asked for it.

On a family vacation to Cyprus, George and his cousin once stole a small supply of food and stored it away. They were certain that no one was wise to their little scheme, until a strange man arrived at their house and dumped all of the stolen goods in front of Mrs. Panos! George received a thorough thrashing from his mother, which, as George told *Sunday* magazine, "certainly taught me a lesson, and I appreciate Mum for teaching me what is right and what is wrong."

Although Mrs. Panos preferred that George spend his time studying instead of rehearsing with Andrew, she would usually give in and let them practice at her house anyway. Once, when she tried again to cool down George's interest in music, he threatened to move out rather than break up his partnership with Andrew. From that point on, Mrs. Panos understood that George's commitment to music was very real.

Andrew Ridgeley grew up with his share of family squabbles, like everybody else. Andrew's younger brother Paul thinks of Andrew this way: "He's very cunning and will always win an argument. There's always been a lot of competition between us . . ." The competition of their childhood years may well continue into adulthood—Paul has *his own* pop band called Physique.

"Andrew Ridgeley grew up with his share of family squabbles, like everybody else."

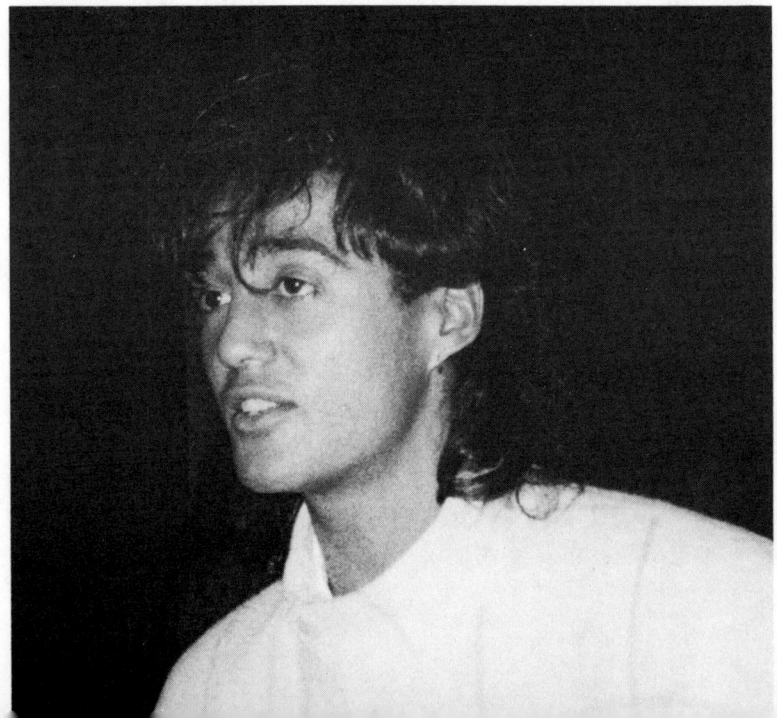

Both George and Andrew are quite earnest in their desire to make money. (After all, George was *never* given an allowance as a boy—his mother would make him cut the lawn or wash the car before she ever gave him any money.)

"We're in the business of selling records. It's not just a matter of getting to #1," George told *Sunday*. "If you're not going to do it properly then it's just not worth bothering. We go straight for the main market. In fact, we're just like our fans—except that we've got more money. But our values and the things that we want and like are the same."

Wham! is well aware that their audience consists of primarily young teenagers. It's also no secret that Wham! songs are written with this age group in mind. Many groups will become immensely popular with teens, but then dismiss their audience as "immature." Likewise, some groups think it hurts their image to be a hit with younger pop audiences. Wham!, on the other hand, likes its teenaged fans and will always try to appeal to them.

One reason teen-oriented pop groups got a bad reputation was that they were usually "manufactured"—that is, put together by a record company to become over-hyped superstars. Bands like the Monkees, the Runaways, or the Bay City Rollers might be considered as such.

George is proud that Wham! has made it as a teen-band entirely on its own terms. As he remarked to *Sunday*, "We're in control of almost everything to do with ourselves—the music, production, songs, artwork, videos, everything."

Some other musicians resent George's honesty about Wham!'s goals as a pop group. "Because we're frank about our moves and motives," George once said, "we're

When it comes to fans, there's no difference between those here and those abroad. Wham! was the first Western pop group ever invited to tour China.

George and Andrew have their differences from time to time, but people often become friends *because* they're different. "I'm definitely a different person without Andrew, and he's a different person without me, and it's whatever comes out of that relationship that is Wham!," George once remarked. Friendship was, and always will be, central to the idea of Wham!, but not just the friendship between George and Andrew. "Most of the friends we had are somehow incorporated into what we're doing now," Andrew says.

With all the pressures of the music business, how can George and Andrew's friendship survive?

As George explained to *Sunday* magazine, "We've always been very close, yet we're not at all similar as characters and have different ambitions." Indeed, Andrew is very straightforward about his ambitions. "I want to be comfortable. I want to do the things that I want to do and half of those things take a lot of money."

An unusual friendship. Many wonder if it will survive sweet success.

Still, Andrew and Paul have strong brotherly ties that are hard to break. "Andy is still very protective toward me," Paul related to *News of the World,* and added that although he's been *bigger* than Andrew since age eleven, "He can't help seeing me as his little brother."

Clearly, George and Andrew care deeply for their families. In fact, for most of their pop music careers, they've continued to live with their parents. Despite the fortune that Wham! has generated, Andrew is still reluctant to move away from home. "Being used to a house that's always been lived in," he told *Rolling Stone,* "starting one from scratch is going to be strange."

George moved out of the house when he bought the Berkshire mansion of the late English film star, Diana Dors. In *Sunday* magazine, George anticipated the reaction this way: "I think Mum'll be heartbroken. She won't actually say so, but I can tell she doesn't want me to leave. I'll miss home, and Mum, of course."

Even though the extraordinary friendship of George and Andrew is recognized all around the world, they've been reported to sharply disagree and even fight in the media. When on tour in the Orient, George and Andrew gave an interview to *Honey* magazine that proved they sometimes drove each other crazy. "You want to say something to him, you have to give him a belt to get his attention," Andrew complained of George. "When we're going on for a show, we've got to wait for him to do his hair."

To that, George replied that his partner lacked tolerance, and added that "the list is endless" of Andrew's other failings. Paul Ridgeley has also been publicly critical of his brother. "Andy can be terribly fickle and callous," he told *News of the World.* "He hurts people without realizing it, and even when he does realize, he doesn't give a damn."

blowing everybody else's cover. It's like we've broken some unspoken code of behavior."

Wham! *has* broken some rules in the past, and will probably continue to do so in the future, but they probably won't forget their friends and family.

As just one example, everyone expected Wham! to celebrate the #1 status of "Wake Me Up before You Go-Go" with a traditional record-industry party at a trendy London nightspot. George and Andrew held *their* party at the North London restaurant run by Mr. Jack Panos!

VIDEO WHAM!

In pop music today, video clips are a necessity. Some performers chafe at the notion of lip-syncing their songs in front of an unfriendly camera. For a group that makes as striking a physical impression as Wham!, the opportunity to star in a music video was ideal. George and Andrew felt there was no reason to fret over their video if they made their motto "enjoy what you do."

George and Andrew's video debut came with "Wham Rap," an inexpensive project by subsequent standards, but its disco setting was appropriate for the lyrics. More ambitious was the "Bad Boys" video concept. George and Andrew originally intended for it to be a kind of takeoff on *West Side Story*—filled with tough characters and gritty street scenes. To the misfortune of Wham!, Michael Jackson's "Beat It" (a video on a very similar theme) was popular at the time and well overshadowed the lower-budgeted "Bad Boys."

In "Young Guns (Go for It!)," George and Andrew are again at a disco with their elegant friends Dee and Shirley. In keeping with the theme of marital instability, young marrieds Andrew and Shirley decide that their differences can't be resolved. George and Andrew ultimately leave the girls, off in search of newer discos and other girlfriends.

Fans at New York's Beacon Theatre.

George and Andrew certainly couldn't complain about having to make the "Club Tropicana" clip—it was filmed at the Spanish resort of Ibiza. Much of it was shot at a luxury hotel, with constant companions Dee and Shirley playing airline stewardesses. The "Club Tropicana" clip ends very much as "Young Guns" does, with George and Andrew abandoning the girls once again.

It was Wham!'s fifth video, "Wake Me Up before You Go-Go," that proved George and Andrew to be as clever in front of a camera as they are in the studio. The bright, clean melody was represented by singers and dancers in white, giant-letter T-shirts that said "CHOOSE LIFE" and assorted colorful attire. The 300 extras who make up the audience in "Wake Me Up" had been forewarned to wear "something white and carry something fluorescent."

VIDEO WHAM! 47

Fluorescent paints and makeup were sometimes worn by hippies in the late 1960s. When an ultraviolet light (sometimes called a black light) is shone on something fluorescent, it glows brilliantly. The celebrated light shows of the 1960s would often use a black light and fluorescent (or Day-Glo) paints.

In the same way that George brought back the girl group sounds of that era, he brought the black light back with him! At one point in the video, an ultraviolet light is shone on the band, and we see them decorated with colorful Day-Glo symbols. (In the 1960s they might have had flowers painted on their faces.)

Wham! showed that a fresh-looking video could actually increase a song's popularity. Still, the "Wake Me Up" clip was not a big-budget affair—it was all shot on one set at home in England.

George attends British Rock-Pop Awards with girlfriend, Pat Hernandez.

For the next video, George Michael went to the opposite extreme. "Careless Whisper" was shot on location and had a plot all its own. Except for a brief glimpse of a hand strumming an acoustic guitar, no one is seen playing an instrument in the entire video.

Shot in Miami, Florida, "Careless Whisper" tells a story that George claims actually happened to him. He's seen cavorting with his girlfriend—in the hotel, in the marina, all over Miami. Before long, a mysterious woman enters the scene and seduces George. The girlfriend discovers George with the glamorous woman and promptly leaves him. George tries to catch up to her, but she has already made her departure by—of all novel things—seaplane. For the rest of the video, George wanders around disconsolately, implying that his mystery woman has left as well. Of course, if this really *did* happen to George, it couldn't have been very long before he found *another* girlfriend!

In "Careless Whisper," the Miami footage that told the story was interspersed with segments of George singing alone on an empty stage. The shots of George singing had been done in England before the whole crew packed off to Miami for the rest of the filming.

Once in Miami, George decided that his hair was too long—even though he needed to keep it the same length it had been back in Britain for the video. As he told *No. 1*, "My sister was with me and she cut my hair on the spot. That haircut cost me £17,000 [over $20,000] because that's how much I went over budget. I've got the most expensive haircut in the history of pop!" George's shorter hair style meant that the entire film crew had to reshoot everything they'd done back in England!

All of Wham!'s videos were directed by Duncan Gibbens and produced by John Roseman. Except for "Young Guns (Go for It!)," all the Wham! videos are included in a package called *WHAM! The Video*, released on CBS/Fox Video. The video set also features "Last Christmas," a clip that has only recently been shown in the United States. As any sensible Wham!-watcher would guess, their videos broke records just as their songs had. British distributors shipped 50,000 copies of *WHAM! The Video*, making it second only to Michael Jackson's *Thriller* in total home video sales!

Are those real tears George is crying as he accepts the British music industry's top award - The Ivor Novello Songwriter of the Year.

THE WHAM! IMAGE

Anyone who follows Wham! knows that style has always been of the utmost importance to them. From their leather-jacketed "Bad Boys" days, to their Fila Sportswear period, to the giant-letter WHAM! T-shirts, Andrew and George can make a style their own. Frankie Goes to Hollywood seemed to be the sole beneficiary of British designer Katherine Hamnett's T-shirts with oversized messages, many of which bear the legend "FRANKIE SAYS . . ." But when George and Andrew put the messages "WHAM!," "CHOOSE LIFE," or "GO-GO" on these big shirts, people soon associated the giant-letter style with Wham!

Although clothing styles have had an impact on Wham!'s popularity, the *life-styles* of George and Andrew have a lot to say about why they mean so much to their fans. Like most of us, George and Andrew didn't grow up with wealthy backgrounds any more than they came from poor households. Their upbringing was comfortably middle-class. As George told *Rolling Stone*, "The stability of both our backgrounds has got a lot to do

THE WHAM! IMAGE

with the fact that a lot of what we do is straight down the middle of the road."

Being middle-class is fine, Wham! seems to say, and so is being *young*. "We're both young," George remarked to the *New Musical Express*. "We've written about what you go through when you're young." Andrew also spoke of the need for this kind of message: "The trouble over the past few years is that the kids are trying to relate to bands that are more *adult* than they want to be."

Despite the fact that George and Andrew have reached full-blown teen-idol status, they're still more interested in keeping themselves amused than in taking themselves seriously. "I suppose there are some blokes who don't like the fact that we play up to the girls," George is quoted as saying in *Wham! In Their Own Words*, "but most of the blokes have a laugh and like it. It's a case of us going, 'Look at the girls screaming at us.' Everything we do is tongue in cheek. I think people should see immediately that it's all a bit of a joke to us."

Suzan Colon is an editor at *Star Hits* magazine, and was one of the few journalists to meet with Wham! during their brief New York stopover in early 1985. What are her strongest impressions of Wham!? "They've got a big reputation for being teases," Suzan related. "For the tour, they had a deejay opening up for them who constantly shouted their names to get audience reaction up. They're big on the tease factor."

Does Wham! do it all for a laugh? "Yeah, they really do look at it like that," replied Suzan. "Especially George. George will do anything for a laugh—everything with him is a real send-up. He does things to annoy people and at the same time shock people, but when *he* says 'shocking,' it's not Boy George–type shocking. It's just to make Wham! more noticed. Whether it's either good or bad—as long as you get the notice—with him it's okay."

With friends Elton John (above) and with Liza Minnelli.

What did she think the *real* George Michael and Andrew Ridgeley were like? "I think they're too honest to be hiding anything," Suzan explained. "I think they're pretty nice guys. In instances when they didn't have to be nice *to me*, they were pretty nice all-around. And usually, when they have something derogatory on their minds, they'll just spit it out. That's part of the George Michael plan, to be completely honest."

Still, when Suzan Colon bade farewell to George, his reaction was surprising. As Suzan remembered, "I tapped him on the shoulder to say 'Goodbye and thanks for everything,' and he whirled around and he said 'Oh, I'm so glad to see you!' and he just threw an arm around me and kissed me on the cheek! I was afraid to go up to him because of all the bigwigs and all that, but what a reception *I* got!"

WHAM! TODAY

Stardom.

That's the only word that can describe the level of success achieved by George Michael and Andrew Ridgeley of Wham! As twenty-two-year-olds, George and Andrew have sold *10,000,000* records worldwide!

Stardom was always part of George and Andrew's grand design, but there were a few things nobody prepared them for, like the time an adoring fan stuck her arm in their limousine door. "Oh, that scares the bloody 'ell out of me," George told *Star Hits*, "If we'd closed that door, her arm would've gone KKKKKRRRKKK!" Andrew agrees, "Bloody terrifying, innit?"

At the other extreme, success often breeds distrust. When Wham! hit it big, some of their earliest fans acted as though the group had "sold out." "If you're going to be successful, you've got to keep quiet about it," George said, "because success does not go hand-in-hand with credibility." When asked if he cared that his credibility was being questioned, George replied, "There's a certain amount of credibility in selling a million records. When you're selling that amount, why do you need people who don't understand what you're doing?"

As Suzan Colon commented on the Wham! partnership, George could probably do it all on his own if he wanted to. "God knows, he's got the talent and everything. He's always successful. . . . But I think that Andrew is his best friend in the entire world and they've been together for years and years and he just wants to take him with him. It rounds out the balance."

Wham! manager Simon Napier-Bell described the alliance in different terms: "It's that extraordinary relationship, like Butch Cassidy and the Sundance Kid, that's been done so many times in the movies, but never before in pop music. The two guys who are incredibly close . . . at the end of the movie, one's got the girl and the other's married, but they still ride off together."

Nonetheless, Napier-Bell thinks Wham! has a lot more than camaraderie going for it. "Kids look at Wham! and say, 'I'd like to be like that.' Parents look at them and say, 'I'd like my children to be like that.' When those two generations come together, you have mammoth acts. . . . In England, only the Beatles have ever done it before."

George and Andrew's parents, initially skeptical of the boys' musical talent, eventually realized what the two had been struggling for. George's father, who used to

Onstage at New York City's Beacon Theatre.

worry that music would make a poor living for his son, is getting to enjoy Wham!'s notoriety. "Now he can see some result," George told the *New Musical Express*, "see me in the papers and on the telly and hear people talking about large amounts of money. He's not worried anymore." Wham! is not fully absorbed in helping themselves, though.

In 1984 and 1985, England endured a crippling miners' strike. The British government stood on one side of the debate and the striking coal miners on the other. Even though the strike was a political powderkeg, some pop musicians gave free concerts to benefit the families of strikers who could no longer pay their bills.

Wham! was one group that heard the call. "All we knew was that there were families caught in the middle of that situation who didn't have enough food," George said.

"We didn't do it for political reasons," Andrew quickly added.

In this same spirit of charity, George Michael joined dozens of his fellow British pop musicians in Band Aid, a group organized to raise money for the relief of drought-stricken Ethiopia. George can be heard on the record and seen in the video clip of the stirring "Do They Know It's Christmas?"

Wham! really *has* made it big. After years of obscurity and unemployment, Wham! is established and respected. The after-school adventures of two trouble-prone friends had changed into a style of music that made the world their dance floor. George Michael and Andrew Ridgeley had a dream that they could take their place among pop music's brightest stars—and the power of their friendship turned that dream into a reality.

◀ *George and Andrew at work on a song - could it be their next big hit?*

FUN FACTS

• To get into shape for their first tour, George and Andrew would play as many games of badminton as they could.

• Andrew's favorite rock 'n' roll album is *Flesh and Blood* by Roxy Music.

• Rumors that David Austin had thrown a champagne bucket at Andrew's nose, breaking it, were entirely false. Andrew's nose was bandaged after minor cosmetic surgery to straighten it out.

• George and Andrew have taken their parents along on every international tour they've ever played.

• The first concert George ever saw was Elton John at Earl's Court in London in 1975.

• When *Star Hits* asked George what he thought about making a fortune in the music industry, he said: "This has got to be one of the only businesses in the world where that can happen so quickly. Suddenly you're in a position where you have as much money as you need, you feel secure, and you have no one to answer to. It's absolutely brilliant! What better job could you have than that?"

• Wham! is the first pop band from a Western nation allowed to perform in the People's Republic of China. They played two concerts there in April 1985—one in Peking and one in Canton. "Careless Whisper" has been translated into both Mandarin and Cantonese dialects of Chinese, and is performed by five different groups!

- Ham and mayonnaise is one of George's favorite sandwiches. Actually, George will eat just about anything if it's smothered in mayonnaise.

- Yog is Andrew's nickname for George.

- When asked if he feels the need to compete with other British groups, George answered: "I'm fed up with all the slagging that goes on. I mean, people make out there's a war between us, Culture Club, and Duran, but we don't think there is. Duran will have a new single out soon, which is bound to go high in the charts. Well, I hope it's really good!"

- It's one of Andrew's great ambitions to become a race-car driver. He was thrilled to meet Formula One driver Derek Warwick when Wham! was in France recording *Making It Big*.

- George Michael is the first pop musician to have two #1 records in the same year, as both a solo artist and as part of a band. The songs were "Wake Me Up before You Go-Go" with Wham! and "Careless Whisper" by himself.

- When asked by *Bop* if he and Andrew ever became interested in the same girl, George responded: "We never fall out over one girl because we go for different sorts of girls. Andrew likes the tall slender ones that I think are skinny and I prefer the more rounded and filled-out ones."

- The restaurant owned by George's father in Edgeware, England now plays *only* Wham! records (and sometimes concert tapes) for its patrons.

VITAL STATISTICS

GEORGE MICHAEL

FULL NAME	George Michael Panos (originally Panayiotou)
BIRTHDATE	June 6, 1963
BIRTHPLACE	London, England
SIGN	Gemini
MARITAL STATUS	single
HEIGHT	6'
WEIGHT	160 lbs.
EYE COLOR	light brown
HAIR COLOR	brown

ANDREW RIDGELEY

FULL NAME	Andrew John Ridgeley
BIRTHDATE	January 26, 1963
BIRTHPLACE	Surrey, England
SIGN	Aquarius
MARITAL STATUS	single
HEIGHT	6'2"
WEIGHT	170 lbs.
EYE COLOR	brown
HAIR COLOR	brown

DISCOGRAPHY AND VIDEOGRAPHY

ALBUMS

FANTASTIC   Innervision/CBS; 1982
Bad Boys
A Ray of Sunshine
Love Machine
Wham Rap (Enjoy What You Do)
Club Tropicana
Nothing Looks the Same in the Light
Come On
Young Guns (Go For It!)

Make It Big   Columbia; 1984
Wake Me Up Before You Go-Go
Everything She Wants
Heartbeat
Like a Baby
Freedom
If You Were There
Credit Card Baby
Careless Whisper

Singles

"Wham Rap (Enjoy What You Do)" backed with "Wham Rap (Club Mix)"   Innervision/CBS; 1982

"Young Guns (Go For It!)" backed with "Going For It"   Innervision/CBS; 1982

"Bad Boys" backed with "Bad Boys (Instrumental)"   Innervision/CBS; 1982

"Club Tropicana" backed with "Blue (Armed with Love)"	Innervision/CBS; 1983
"Club Fantastic Megamix"; "A Ray of Sunshine"; "Come On"; "Love Machine"	Innervision/CBS; 1983
"Wake Me Up Before You Go-Go" backed with "Wake Me Up Before You Go-Go (Instrumental)"	Columbia; 1984
"Careless Whisper" backed with "Careless Whisper (Instrumental)"	Columbia; 1984
"Freedom" backed with "Freedom (Instrumental)"	Columbia; 1984
"Everything She Wants" backed with "Like a Baby"	CBS; 1985
"Last Christmas" backed with "Everything She Wants"	Columbia; 1985

VIDEOS

Wham Rap (Enjoy What You Do)
Young Guns (Go For It!)
Bad Boys
Club Tropicana
Wake Me Up Before You Go-Go
Careless Whisper
Everything She Wants
Last Christmas

WRITE TO WHAM!

c/o Columbia Records

1801 Century Park West
Los Angeles, CA 90067

OR

c/o Nomis Management
17 Gosfield St.
London WI
ENGLAND